WEE FOLKS STORIES

FROM

THE OLD TESTAMENT

WEE FOLKS STORIES

FROM

THE OLD TESTAMENT

MOSTLY IN WORDS OF ONE SYLLABLE

Elizabeth Robinson Scovil

Updated by Jonathan Savage, Esq.
Edited by Mikesch Muecke, Ph.D.

Hog Press
an imprint of Culicidae Press
PO Box 5069
Madison, WI 53705-5069
USA
hogpress.com
editor@hogpress.com
+1 (352) 388-3848
+1 (515) 462-0278

WEE FOLKS STORIES FROM THE OLD TESTAMENT: MOSTLY IN WORDS OF ONE SYLLABLE
2023 © Elizabeth Robinson Scovil

All rights reserved. No part of this work covered by the copyright hereon may be reproduced or used in any form or by any means— graphic, electronic, or mechanical, including photocopying, recording, taping, or information storage and retrieval systems— without written permission of the publisher. Neither the author nor the publisher make any representation, express or implied, with regard to the accuracy of the information contained in this book and cannot accept any legal responsibility or liability for any errors or omissions that may be made.

ISBN: 978-1-941892-76-3

Our books may be purchased in bulk for promotional, educational or business use. Please contact your local bookseller or the Hog Press Sales Department at +1-515-462-0278 or email us at sales@hogpress.com

twitter.com/culicidaepress – facebook.com/culicidaepress

Book layout and design by polytekton ©2023, based on the original by Elizabeth Robinson Scovil
Background photo on cover by Félix Bonfils (1831-1885), *General View of Jerusalem* [*Vue générale de Jérusalem*]

Table of Contents

Preface	6
The World is Made	9
Man Sins	11
Cain and Abel	14
The Ark	16
The Two Boys	19
Isaac's Wife	21
The Twin Sons	24
The Bad Brothers	27
Joseph in Egypt	30
The Famine	33
Joseph's Plan	35
The Baby in the Nile	38
The Ten Plagues	41
The Red Sea	43
Samuel	46
The Shepherd King	49
King Solomon	51
Náaman	54
Daniel	57
Coloring Pages	60-73

Preface

The original of this text was written by Ms. Elizabeth Robinson Scovil, and was published and copyrighted in 1920. Jonathan found the original 1920 version in his mother's belongings.

The book was re-printed in the early 1930s.

Ms. Scovil's intent was to write a book of mostly one syllable words so that the youngest of children (the 'wee folks') could better hear, read and understand the messages from some favorite and critical Old Testament stories.

The text and pictures of this book mirror Ms. Scovil's original publication, with only a few changes to reflect our contemporary language. Truly, this is her book one-hundred-and-three years after her original publication.

Ms. Scovil (1849 – 1934) was a truly remarkable woman for the ages. To learn more about Ms. Elizabeth Robinson Scovil, go to http://bit.ly/scovil

The original title of this book was *Wee Folks Stories From The Old Testament – In Words of One Syllable,* a title we kept while adding the word 'Mostly' because there are some required two-syllable words in the text as well.

Jonathan dedicates the efforts related to this book to his grandchildren, and the children and grandchildren of Jonathan's sister Judy, his brother Rick, and his adoptive sister Joy. Joy is now in heaven.

Mikesch dedicates the efforts related to this book to his family, his partner, and her children and grandchildren.

The World is Made

God made the world in which we live full of joy for us: The green grass that grows in the spring, the pink buds that peep out when the sun shines and the air is warm; the bright red leaves that come when the green ones change, and then fall to the ground when the trees go to sleep late in the year; the clear ice and the clean white snow that lies on it in all the north-lands when the air is cold and frost is here.

Once there were none of these things to be seen. The earth was dark and still. Then God made the sun to shine in the day and the moon and the stars to give light at night. Rain and dew fell, and plants grew to give us food, and fruit formed, ripe and sweet, for us to eat.

Birds came to sing and make nests in the trees. Sheep and cows, with their lambs and calves, strayed in the fields and fed on the grass. Beasts roamed in the fields. Fish swam in the sea and the streams. Bees hummed in the soft air. Ants dug their cells in the rich earth. All things that move, that can run, or fly, or swim, were full of joy in life.

The deep blue sky, with its soft white clouds, like the lambs' fleece of wool, looked down on the green earth. The sunlight danced on the lakes and ponds. At night the moon, or the stars, shone on each still place, where all slept, and none felt fear, for all were safe.

There was no one to see and use all these good things, so God made a man and put him in the midst of them. He called him Adam. That Adam might have a help-meet for him, someone to share them with, God gave him a wife, whose name was Eve, to be with him.

Man Sins

In the place where God had put Adam and Eve there was one tree whose fruit God told them not to touch — if they ate it, they would die. Eve did not know what death meant. No one had died yet, so she did not fear it as much as she would have done if she had seen death. The fruit was ripe and full of juice, and she longed to taste it. One day a bad spirit in the shape of a snake told Eve that she could eat the fruit if she cared to, for it was not true that she would die. She took the fruit, and gave some to Adam, who ate it too.

God was grieved that when He had made all these good things for them and done so much for them, they would not do the one small thing He had asked them to do. He could not leave them in the fair place where He had put them at first, as He could not trust them. He sent

them out into a land where things did not grow on their own, and they had to work to get food to eat.

They had no clothes, so Eve joined fig leaves and sewed them to make a kind of dress for them. By and by God gave them clothes made of the skins of beasts to keep them warm.

They could not go back. God placed an angel at the gate with a bright sword to keep them out. They had to stay where they were. The glad days were gone when they could get what they liked without hard work.

Cain and Abel

In time Adam and Eve had two sons, named Cain and Abel. When some years had passed, a third son named Seth was born. Abel took care of flocks of sheep. Cane worked on the land, and made things grow, as they do on farms.

One day Abel brought a lamb of his flock to give it to God. Cain brought some of the things that he had raised, grain, or fruit to give God too. God saw that Abel's heart was full of love for Him, and he gave the best he had to show it. Cain brought his things without love; he thought he had to give them, but it was not love that moved him to do it. God took Abel's gift and blessed him. He would not take Cain's gift — there was no love to make it sweet to Him.

Cain was filled with rage when he found God would not have what he had brought; his face grew dark and cross. He did not blame his own lack of love. He blamed

Abel. Hard words lead to blows; Cain struck Abel and Abel died.

God told Cain that as he had killed Abel, a mark would be put on his face, so that all would know he had killed a man; but they must not kill Cain. When he worked hard to make things grow out of the ground, it would not yield large crops as it used to do for him. Then, too, God told him he would have no home on earth.

Cain must have wished he had not let his rage make him kill Abel. Now it was too late.

The Ark

Long years had passed since Cain's death. Men had ceased to love God or to want to please Him, and so things had grown bad. God said: He would send a great flood and drown all but a few in this world. He meant to save these, so the whole race would not die out from this. He told the man named Noah to build an ark that would float like a kind of large ship and in it Noah was to put two of all things that had life, to keep them safe from the flood. Noah did as God told him and built the ark and filled it. He took his wife in it with him and three sons and their wives. It rained for forty days and nights.

All that breathed the breath of life outside of the ark were drowned. The flood kept up for five months.

Then Noah sent out a dove to see if she could find dry land. When she came back with a leaf in her mouth, Noah knew the dove must have picked it off a tree. The next

time Noah sent her out she did not come back. She had found a dry place where she could stay. So, Noah and all that were in the ark with him, left the ark.

God told Noah that He would set God's colorful bow in the cloud, so that when it rained hard and Noah feared a flood might come, he would see the the bright bow and know he need not fear. We see the bow still sometimes when it rains, and we call it a 'rainbow.'

The Two Boys

Noah's first son was named Shem, and when a great while had passed, Abraham was born. When Abraham grew up, he was such a good man. He was called the 'Friend of God'.

Abraham's wife was named Sarah. She was most fair to see and all loved to look at her, but she had no child. This was a great grief to her, and when she was quite old, she prayed to God that He would send her a son. God gave her the wish of her heart, and sent her a son. His name was Isaac which means 'one who laughs and rejoices'.

God said: He would do great things for Isaac. Abraham gave a great feast. He had a son named Ishmael, a name that means 'God will hear'. This boy made fun of Sarah and her child and teased them. Sarah was so upset. She said that Ishmael and his mother Hagar must be sent away. She would not let them live near her and her son, so Abraham sent them off, but he gave Hagar bread and something to drink that she and her boy would not starve.

They went straight into a wild place where there was no food, and where no one lived to help them. Hagar feared that she and her son would starve to death, and she hid her face, so she should not see her boy die. God sent one of his angels to help her and show her where she could find a drink and food for herself and her son. God took care of them until Ishmael was a man.

Isaac's Wife

When Isaac grew up, Abraham did not want to choose a wife from the girls in the land where he lived. They did not know the true God. So, he told one of his men to go to the land Abraham had come from and bring a wife from there for his son. The man said: the girl might not want to come back with him. Abraham was sure God would put it in the heart of the right girl to come, and so it turned out.

The man who went had ten camels to carry his goods, for he took a load of gifts for the girl who would be Isaac's wife. It was near the end of the day when he came to a town. There was a water well where the girls from the town came at this time of day. He made his great beasts kneel down so they could drink. Then he asked God to give him a sign to show him which girl would be the best wife for Isaac. When he said to one of them 'Let down the cup that I may drink', and if she said 'Drink and I will give thy

camels drink too', he would know that she was the one God chose to go home with him. Rebecca was the name of the fair girl who said to him: "Drink, my lord." And when he asked her, she helped with the camels too. He found that she was one of Abraham's own. She went back with him to be Isaac's so much-loved wife.

The Twin Sons

Isaac and Rebekah had twin sons, Esau and Jacob. One day Esau came in from the field, and was weak from lack of food. Jacob had made a dish of a kind of red beans that smelled good to Esau, and he longed to taste it. Jacob said to Esau that if he would give to Isaac all Esau's rights as the first-born, he could have the food to eat. Esau thought he might as well give up his birth rights as to wait until he could get food. Esau might not like it as well later, so he swore that he would give up his first-born rights. God had made him the first-born, but Esau did not care much for his birth-right.

Years passed and Isaac was an old man soon to die, and he was blind. He meant to bless Esau — his first-born son. Rebecca wished him to bless Isaac, that he might be a great man on earth. Isaac would not slight Esau, and she did not see how she could have her way.

Isaac called Esau to him one day and told him when he went to hunt to bring some wild goat meat and cook it for him, that he might eat it and bless him. Rebecca heard this and told Jacob to kill two good goats of their flock, and she would cook them so Isaac would like them and would not want the meat Esau brought. She put the skin of the goats on Jacob's smooth neck and hands, so Isaac would not know him, for Esau's neck and hands had hair on them, and she dressed him in Esau's clothes.

Jacob took bread and the goat meat to Isaac, and when Isaac felt him, he said: "The hands are the hands of Esau, but the voice is the voice of Jacob," and thought he was Esau the first-born, and so he blessed him.

When Esau came home and found he was too late, he gave a great cry and cried salt tears and said that he would kill Jacob. He did not think of the day that he sold his birth-right and that it was his own fault.

Jacob did not want to do this wrong thing, but Rebecca forced him to do it. Do you think he tried as hard as he might have done to do right?

The Bad Brothers

Jacob had two wives, Leah and Rachel. The first one had ten sons, the second two sons, Joseph and Benjamin. And these were the two that Jacob loved the most.

The sons of the first wife were not kind to the two young boys. They thought Jacob loved Joseph too much; Jacob made Joseph a coat of bright stripes and called him the son of his old age.

One day Jacob sent Joseph to see the ten, who had gone to feed their flock of sheep in a far place. When they saw him, they said: "Come now. let us kill him and cast him in some pit and we will say some fierce beast ate him up." One of them named Ruben said: "Let us not kill him, but throw him in the pit." Ruben meant to come back and get Jacob out when the brothers were gone.

They took off Joseph's bright coat and cast him in the pit. Some men passed that way and took Joseph out and sold him to a band of Ishmaelites, who took him with them to Egypt.

When Ruben came back to save Joseph, he was gone. Then they dipped Joseph's coat in the blood of a goat and took the coat home to Jacob. They told him a wild beast had killed his boy.

When he saw the coat and blood, poor Jacob said: "Without doubt, Joseph is dead." He mourned and wept for his son a long time. He loved him so much, he said his grief would last until he went down in his own grave. All the while Joseph was safe in Egypt.

Joseph in Egypt

In the course of years, Joseph rose to be a great man in Egypt. At first, he was sold as a slave, but the man who bought him was kind to him. Joseph was so good and worked so hard that God blessed Joseph, and all that he did, turned out well. He grew rich, for he was well paid, and he had full charge of all that was in the house and in the fields of the man who owned him, who was one of the king's guards.

As time passed, the wife of this man did not treat Joseph well. She said: Joseph was not true to the man. The man, of course, thought his wife spoke the truth, and he put Joseph in jail. But God was still with Joseph. In the jail, there were two men who had served the king — one baked the bread for the king's house, and the other used to wait on the king when he was at meals. Each of these men dreamed a dream, and Joseph told them what the

dreams meant. The first man was to be hanged, and the second was to be set free to wait on the king once more. When the king heard what Joseph had said, he thought he should like to see him and hear what the king's own dreams meant. When two years had passed the king sent for Joseph. The king was so pleased with Joseph's words, and found him such a wise and good man, so the king said: Joseph should rule the whole land of Egypt. The king took off his own ring and put it on Joseph's hand and put a gold chain on Joseph's neck.

The Famine

There was a real need for food in all the lands. The crops failed, and there was no grain to grind into flour to make bread. Joseph knew this time of need would come, for God had told him. So, he bought food and stored it to have it to sell when there was none else to be had. A part of all the food that was growing in the good years was stored in this way. When the years of no food came, all cried to the king for bread. He said, go to Joseph and do what he says to do. Joseph took the grain out of his stores and sold it to those who came.

Men came from the other lands to buy corn, for they had no food. When Jacob heard that there was corn in Egypt, he told his sons to go to Egypt and buy food so that they may live and not die. So, they went down to buy bread — these were the men who had thrown Joseph in the pit and thought he was dead. They did not know that except for the king, none was so great as Joseph in all the land of Egypt. As a boy, the brothers had tried to kill Joseph. They were told they would have to see Joseph, as no food could be sold without his yes. They went and stood in front of him, and bowed low, each with his face to the Earth. Joseph knew them at once, though they did not know him.

Joseph longed to hear if Jacob still lived, and if Benjamin had grown up. So, he asked them these things and much more.

Joseph's Plan

At last Joseph thought of a plan to see Benjamin.

He said: to the men "you are spies and have come to see how bare the land is." They said: "We are not spies my lord. We are true men". Joseph said: "If you are true men, you must stay here and one of you shall go and bring Benjamin for me to see." They did not want to do this, so Joseph just put them all in jail. In three days, they thought it best to go. Simeon stayed bound in jail. Joseph had their sacks filled with grain, and the money they had brought to pay, for it was put in the mouth of each sack as it was laid on the back of the donkeys and they set off.

When they got home, they said: to Jacob, the man who is the lord of the land, was rough with them and took them as spies. "We told him who we were and about you and Benjamin. He said that we must come back and bring

Benjamin to him. Jacob did not want to let Benjamin go, but Ruben, who had tried to save Joseph when he was a lad, said that he would take good care of Benjamin and bring him back safely.

At last Jacob said that he would go. When Joseph saw Benjamin, he sent out all who were in the room except the men who had brought Benjamin and told them who he was, and Joseph cried for joy. Then he said that Jacob and all his sons must live in Egypt, where Joseph could take care of them, which they did.

The Baby in the Nile

The king of Egypt gave Jacob the land of Goshen to live in. Then God gave Jacob a new name — Israel, which means 'the prince of God', so all who lived in this land, were called 'the children of Israel'.

In time, the king died and a new king reigned. This king did not know Joseph. The Egyptians feared the Israelites for they grew so strong and great. The Egyptians fought the Israelites and made them slaves.

Like most slaves, the Israelites were treated badly, and made to do all the hard work. To keep them few, the Egyptian king said that each boy born to the Israelites should be killed, so there would be no more men. You can think how sad this made the poor Israelites.

A son was born into the tribe of Levi. He was such a fine child. They took care of him for three months. After three months when they couldn't hide him anymore, they made a small boat of a kind of stout grass that grew in a wet place, and they spread pitch on it to keep it floating. In this they put the tightly wrapped baby. They placed the little boat on the bank of the Nile River. His sister, Miriam, stayed near to see what the end would be.

The king's daughter walked by the Nile that day, and saw the little boat in the weeds. She told her maid to fetch it. When she saw the sweet child, she loved him and longed to save him. Miriam came near and said that she would get someone to nurse the baby for the king's daughter. The daughter said yes, and Miriam brought the baby's mother to take care of him.

The Ten Plagues

The king's daughter called the boy Moses, which means 'drawn out'. Moses was to her as her own son. He grew up to be a wise and great man. One day, God told Moses that he meant to send the children of Israel out of Egypt back to their own land, and that Moses was to lead them.

The king, whose name was Pharaoh, said that the Israelites were his slaves, and he would not let them go. God said that He would do such things in Egypt that Pharaoh would have to let them go. In fact, he would be glad to send them out. Pharaoh laughed. He did not think God could do this.

Then God sent ten plagues on the land. First, Moses stretched out his rod over the Nile and it and all the streams in the Nile turned to blood. The fish died, and no one could drink. Next, a vast herd of frogs swarmed on the land. Third, Moses smote the dust, and it turned into lice that crawled on all things. Then Pharaoh's house was filled with swarms of flies that buzzed in the ears. Fifth, the herds died — cows and calves, sheep, and lambs, the horse and the donkeys laid down, and rose no more. Sixth, Moses filled his hands with ashes, shook it out, and it brought boils out on man and beast. Next, hail fell and spoiled all the crops. Eighth, locusts came and ate all the green things. They were so thick, no one could see the ground. Ninth, it was dark in all the land for three days. Pharaoh could not move from his place, but the children of Israel had light where they lived. The tenth plague was by far the worst of all. God sent his angel to kill the first-born child of all the Egyptians. From the king on down, the first born of both man and beast died. When the night past, there was not a home where there was not one dead. Then Pharaoh said: "Rise up, go ye forth, and go serve the Lord." As he said this, the Egyptians told the Israelites to make haste, or they will all be dead men. The children of Israel went with all they had, and much more when the Egyptians gave them more to get rid of them. The Israelites were free!

The Red Sea

God led the children of Israel through a land of rocks and sand. Where they were, there was no food. A cloud went in front of them by day, and a bright light like fire at night to show them the way. At last, they came to the Red Sea, and Pharaoh said: "Those slaves of mine are lost in that wild land. I will go out and get them and bring them back." When the children of Israel saw the Egyptian soldiers come to them, Moses said: "Fear not and stand still, and see what God will show you this day. The Egyptians have seen this day and they shall see you no more. The Lord shall fight for you, and you shall hold your peace."

God told Moses to lift up his rod and stretch out his hand on the sea and the waves would part some to his right and some to his left and stand like a wall on each side

and have a dry path. Moses did so. The children of Israel walked through on dry land.

The Egyptians rushed on, but a strong east wind drove the waves back and drowned them.

In spite of what God had done for Israel, they grieved Him by their sins. He could not take them at once to the good land God meant to give them. They were not fit to live there.

After many years had passed, Moses and most of those who left Egypt with him had died. At last, God led the Israelites into Canaan.

Samuel

The children of Israel grew rich and great in the land of Canaan, which God gave them in His own good time.

Years passed, a great temple had been built, where people would pray and sing praise to God. One day Eli, who was the priest in charge and served God day and night there, saw the wife of a man, and she had come with him a long way to pray to the Lord of Hosts.

As she knelt in prayer, tears rolled down her cheeks and she was sad. She had no child and she longed for one of her own, so she vowed to God that if He would give her a son, she would send him to live in the temple and give him up to work for God. Eli was near and heard her prayer. He said: "Go in peace, the God of Israel will grant thee what thou hast asked of Him."

When her son came, she called him Samuel, which means 'asked of God'. She took him with her when she went to pray, and told Eli that as long as he lived, Samuel would be lent to the Lord, who gave him to her.

In time, Samuel went to live with Eli to serve God. Each year Hannah, Samuel's mother, made a small coat to fit him and brought it to him. She had three more boys and two girls now.

One night when the child Samuel slept, he was roused by a voice that called his name. He thought Eli spoke, but it was not he. When next he heard it, Eli told him that it was the voice of God, and the third time to say: "Speak Lord for thy child hears."

Samuel did so. God said to tell Eli his sons were not good men and could not be His priest as Eli had hoped. Samuel had to tell Eli the sad news. Poor Eli said: "It is the Lord; let Him do what seems good to Him." Eli knew his sons were not fit to be the priests of God.

Samuel lived to be chief in Israel and judge all the tribes for years. At last, they asked for a king; God told Samuel to choose Saul, the son of Kish, a fine young man, to rule them. Samuel poured oil on Saul's head and blessed him and made him king.

The Shepherd King

Saul did prove to be neither a wise nor good king. At last God told Samuel to choose someone else to be king in place of Saul. The choice Samuel made was a young man named David, who all his life had cared for a flock of sheep. He had red cheeks, a bright face, and was good to look at. God knew he was brave and true and would make a good king.

Saul sent for David to come to his court and loved him when he saw him. He did not know that David was one day to be king in his place. Saul had dark, sad thoughts and dwelt too much on them in his mind. When he heard music, it eased his deep gloom, so he liked David to play on the harp and sing to him.

The Israelites were at war. One of the many who fought them was a huge man named Goliath. He was more than ten feet tall. He wore a cap of brass, a coat of mail, brass greaves on his legs and a large shield of brass on his back. In his hand he carried a great spear, like the beam of a loom, and a man walked before him with a huge shield.

David begged Saul to let him try to kill Goliath; he knew God would help him. He took five smooth stones out of a brook and put them in a bag and took his sling in his hand. The huge man laughed at David. David put a stone in a sling and shot the stone at Goliath. It hit Goliath near his eyes and he fell dead.

King Solomon

David had to fight for his throne, and he did not sit on it in peace until Saul was dead. David was much loved by all of Israel, and he lived to be an old, old man. When he was gone, his son Solomon reigned in his place.

God gave Solomon great wealth and a wise mind, so that he judged Israel as well as ruled it.

One day two women brought a child to his court; each claimed the child was her own. Solomon knew they could not both own it, so he said: "Bring a sword and cut the child in two and give half to each." One of the women cried out: "Oh my lord, give her the child; in no wise slay it." The next said: "Let it not be mine or thine but kill it." Then Solomon knew that the first was the mother and he gave the child to her.

There was peace in all the land, and Solomon said: he meant to build a great house to the name of the Lord, so that God might be praised there by all of Israel. It was built of stone, cut and shaped first, so that no sound of ax or tool was heard when it was built. There was much carved wood used, at a great cost, and on a large part of it were laid sheets of pure gold. When it was done, there was no house as grand in all the world.

Solomon reigned long. When he died, Solomon was laid in his grave, which was near David's.

Náaman

The men of Syria were at war with the Israelites. They had made a raid in their land, and had brought back a young maid. She lived in the house of Náaman, a great man in the host of the king of Syria, but he was a sick man. The maid said to Náaman's wife that she was sure that if Náaman would go to Elisha, a man of God in Israel, God would heal him.

Náaman asked the king to write to the king of Israel and tell him that Elisha must cure him. The king of Israel did not know what to do. He said: "Am I God, to kill and to make to live?" When Elisha heard of it, he said: "Let Náaman now come to me, and he shall know that there is a man of God in Israel."

Náaman drove to the door of Elisha's house. Elisha sent out word that the great man was to wash seven times in the Jordan, and he should be clean. Náaman was filled

with rage and went off. He said: "I thought he would be sure to come out to me and stand and call on the name of the Lord his God and strike his hand on the place and make me well. Are not the streams of Damascus as good as the Jordan? May I not wash in them and be clean?"

The men with him begged him to do as Elisha said that it was not a hard thing to do. At last, Náaman went down and dipped seven times in the Jordan, and his flesh became like the flesh of a child, and he was clean. Then he knew that God was the true God and praised Him.

Daniel

Daniel was the son of a prince of the tribe of Judah. The king of Babylon had brought Daniel and three of his friends from one of the king's raids in the land of Israel. This king did not know our God. Daniel kept his faith, and would not pray to strange gods.

Daniel grew wise and the king found that all he said was just and true. He loved Daniel so much, which made the men in the king's court hate Daniel, but as long as the king lived, Daniel was safe. When the king's son came to the throne, Daniel's enemies made up their minds that Daniel should die. They could not find that he had done any wrong, so they begged the king to make a law that no one should ask a thing of God or man for one month but from the king himself. If he did, he should be cast in the den of lions.

When Daniel heard this, he went in the house three times a day and knelt down and prayed to God, as he had been used to. The king wished now that he had not made the law, but for his oath's sake, he had to have Daniel thrown to the wild beasts. He knew Daniel was such a good man that he said to him: "Your God, whom you serve, will save you."

When the sun rose, the king got up and went in haste to the den. Daniel was safe. He said: "Oh King, my God sent his angel and shut the lion's mouths; they have not hurt me, for I had done no wrong." Then the king was glad.

The End

Your child (or you) can color in the images from the book on the next pages. Enjoy!

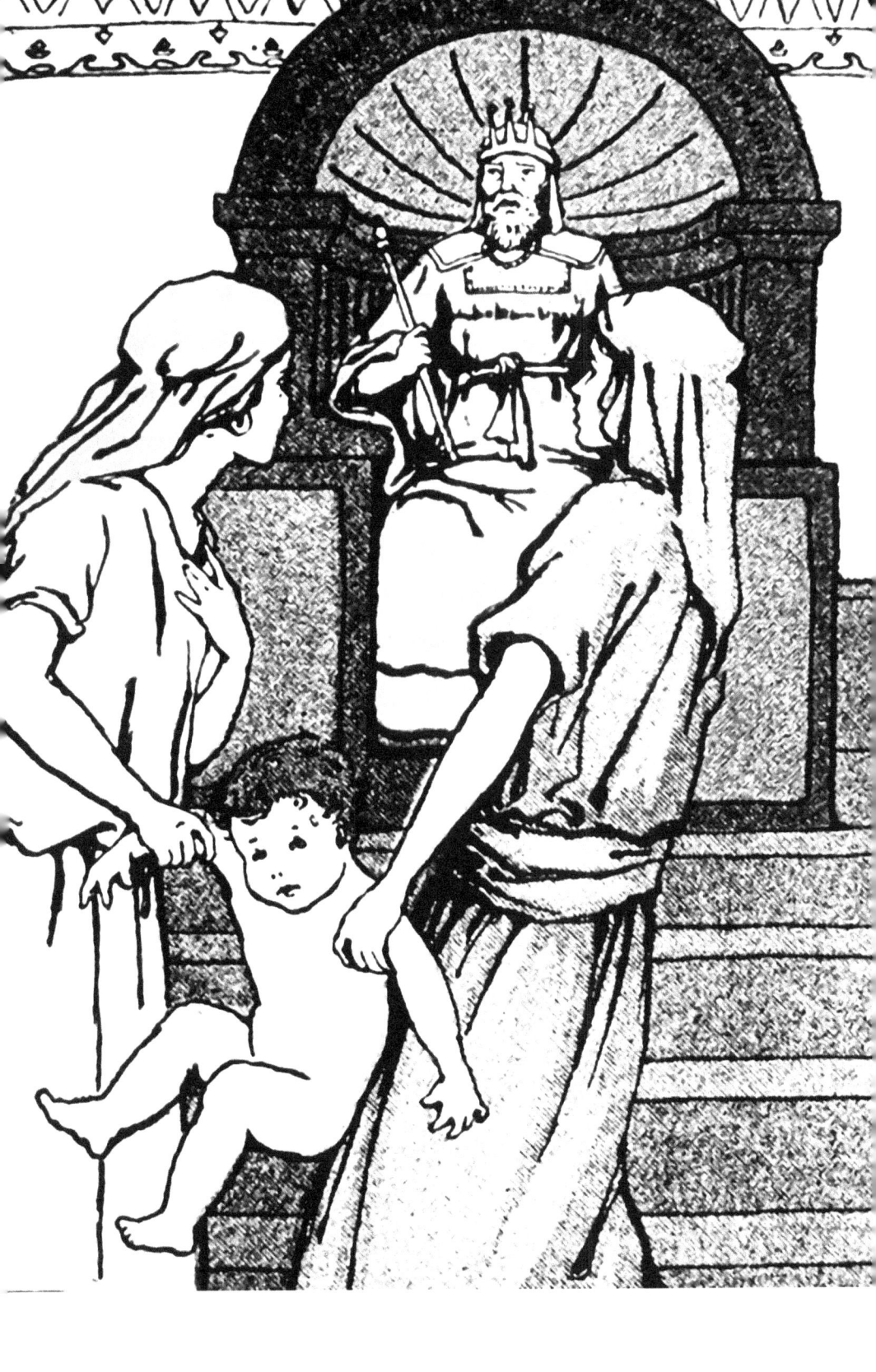

Savage+Berthiaume+Hathcock Press LTD